RUFUS

THE STORY
OF A FOX

RUFUS

THE STORY OF A FOX

ERNEST DUDLEY

FREDERICK MULLER LTD

First published in Great Britain 1971 by
Frederick Muller Ltd., 110 Fleet Street, London, E.C.4

Copyright © Ernest Dudley 1971

Illustrated and designed by Margaret Major

Printed by The Anchor Press Ltd., and
bound by Wm. Brendon & Son Ltd.,
both of Tiptree, Essex
SBN: 584 10237 2

CONTENTS

A SPARED LIFE

CHAPTER ONE

THE two men and their dogs, a collie and a terrier, waited outside the fox's den in the forest above Ballachulish. From the little town along the shore of Loch Leven, lights flickered through the mist that rose off the loch. In the April twilight that was darkening the forest both men and their dogs were concentrated on the entrance to the fox's earth. Somewhere an owl hooted. The moon was beginning to climb through a straggle of fleecy cloud. Scattered stars made a pale twinkle in the sky. Apart from the owl's hoot and the trickle of a nearby burn the forest was silent. The men kept their voices low.

The fox's den had originally been burrowed by rabbits out of the summit of a rocky mound. Above it rowan saplings bent gently to the light wind. Beside the man with the collie the vixen lay, most of her head blasted off by shot; the man held a shotgun under his arm. Her mate, the dog-fox, had died earlier that afternoon, caught in the steel jaws of a trap hidden in the bracken and finished off by the man with the shotgun.

The dog-fox and his vixen were a young pair; the cubs down in the darkness of the den had been their first litter, tiny, mewling furry shapes. When her mate had failed to show up with a rabbit, bird, or mice he had been hunting, the vixen herself had left the den to search for food for her cubs. The men had been waiting for her.

The man with the terrier finished rolling his cigarette. Without taking his eyes off the dark entrance to the den he cupped the flame of a match with his hands. He and the other man spoke in monosyllables. He took his terrier, and as it gave an excited yelp, put its head into the den. It disappeared, stumpy tail wagging. The collie came obediently to heel beside the other man.

Now the terrier's muffled yap could be heard. Its yapping grew louder to the cubs huddled close together in instinctive terror hard against the wall of the earth. The dark earth, once warm and secure for them, was now a death-cell. Above, the men knew by the worrying gurgle from the terrier's throat followed by a sudden silence that it had made its first kill. The collie's tail wagged, he whimpered with suppressed excitement.

The terrier appeared, wagging tail first, dragging out a small, still twitching furry body. The man with the cigarette took it from the terrier, which needed no word to send it back down into the earth once more. The collie whimpered more loudly, the other man spoke sharply, and he quietened. The man with the cub threw it down beside its mother. Before it lay still it gave one final twitch that attracted the collie's attention. The collie's sharp head jerked back to the entrance to the earth. From below, the terrier's muffled yapping. It turned into the growl in the throat again, then silence, followed by the appearance of the wagging tail as another cub was dragged out.

The terrier was already scrabbling its way down for a third kill. The man took a deep pull of satisfaction from his cigarette, the thin spiral of smoke vanishing quickly on the darkening air. Again the terrier backed out with a third twitching, furry shape. The collie whimpered. The moon had climbed out of the straggle of cloud. Back went the terrier. His muffled yelps ascended.

As the terrier dived down into the earth yet again the man with the collie let out an exclamation. With a swift movement he dashed forward, then stepped back, in his hands a ball of struggling fur.

It was a fifth fox-cub. Miraculously it had blundered its way to escape out of the earth by another tunnel. The man stared at it in his hands, while the other took his cigarette from his mouth, spat out a shred of tobacco and reached to grab the cub.

The man shook his head. "Nae, let's spare this yin."

It may have been a sudden compassion for the eager life charging the tiny body in his grip, it may have been a twist of revulsion at the smell of death that reached his nostrils. The cigarette's glow reddened in surprise. The shotgun under his arm, the man held the cub in the curve of his shoulder. As the collie made a leap up, teeth glistening, he cuffed it down with his free hand. "I ken a lad in Ballachulish'll give me ten bob for it," he said.

The other gave a shrug. It was twenty shillings for an adult fox's tail; ten shillings per cub before it leaves its earth. The terrier had turned aside from the entrance to the den; it had made its last kill for that night. The dog-fox, the vixen and the four cubs shoved into a gamekeeper's bag, the man with the cigarette moved off. The terrier trotted after him, nose lifted to the scent from the bag. The man holding the tiny cub called his collie to heel and followed.

Which was how a fox-cub who was to become famous first came to know human beings.

Six months later, early September, 1968.

Meg Allan had learned from Don MacCaskill the night before that he was going over to Ballachulish next afternoon, to see about getting a fox he'd heard of. Meg had lain awake that night staring through her bedroom window at the starlit sky. Would Don MacCaskill really get the fox? What would it be like? Would she be able to hold it in her arms?

She was aged fourteen, the only child of Joe Allan and his wife, Jean. Joe was a gamekeeper on nearby Lock Aweside, renowned for his wily skill as a stalker. The village where Meg lived with her father and mother, no more than nine houses and a school, was called Inverinan. It means the mouth of the River Inan, on whose banks the village stands and which runs into Loch Awe.

Meg hadn't told her father about Don MacCaskill going to Ballachulish to get this fox. Joe Allan had an implacable hatred for foxes. Vermin, they were, that killed pheasants and carried off baby lambs. Rip up a sheep at lambing time, a fox would, just for its milk. Meg's mother sided with him. Murderous, cunning things that would eat every egg, slaughter every fowl in a poultry run in one go. So Meg said nothing to her about Don MacCaskill's trip to Balla-chulish.

Don had received the telephone-call one evening from Mrs Mackenzie who lived at Ballachulish. She had told him that her nephew had this young fox that he would have to get rid of. She'd heard of Don MacCaskill, the forester on Loch Aweside, who was said to be interested in keeping a fox. Yes, Don said, he had been thinking of keeping one. He already had an enclosure ready for it.

Ballachulish is about fifty miles from Inverinan, taking the Oban road, branching right over Connel Bridge and on through Appin along the shores of Loch Linnhe. Don's wife, Catherine, was going with him and said that on the way back they could come through the mountains of Glencoe.

They set off in their Dormobile caravan about mid-day. Catherine thought it would give them time to take it easy and enjoy the loveliest parts of the Western Highlands, the road winding through forest and glen, tiny villages, lochs on either side. But her husband gave no thought to all this. His mind was fixed on the fox. It was all he could do not to exceed a sensible speed, he was so anxious to get there. At the idea of this fox his blood tingled with excitement, he could feel the grin of anticipation on his face, and he had to remember to stop smiling to himself. The fox mightn't be what he expected;

it might be too wild, impossible to tame, or too cowed, all the life whipped out of it.

They crossed Connel Bridge and had a picnic lunch by the roadside over-looking shimmering Loch Creran. You could see the seals, Catherine said, basking in the sunshine on the little isles on the loch. But Don didn't get out the field-glasses he always carried wherever he went. He wasn't interested in the seals, or the white sea swallows swooping over their nests on the rocky islets. He just prayed that the fox would turn out all he wanted it to be. He wanted to talk about it; would it be in good health, or would it be neglected, ill-affected by being in captivity? But his wife had lunch ready and felt hungry.

After lunch they passed through Appin, where Catherine pointed out the ruined tower of Castle Stalker, then the slate roofs of Ballachulish came in sight, making a blueish glint against the forest beyond that towered up to-wards Glencoe. Mrs Mackenzie and her nephew lived on the outskirts of Ballachulish near the village of Glencoe itself.

It was just before five o'clock, and when Don rang at the house in a row of neat, small houses, Mrs Mackenzie said he had arrived too soon. Her nephew wasn't back from work in the forest yet. Don and his wife took a stroll round the village. He managed to conceal the tingle of anticipation as they returned to the house. The nephew—he was named Ian—still hadn't arrived. It had gone five o'clock. But he would be back any minute. No, Don wouldn't like to see the fox while he waited. He preferred to wait for young Mackenzie to intro-duce him, so to speak. A fox, like other animals, doesn't always like meeting a human being who is a complete stranger.

A few minutes later Ian Mackenzie, quiet, pleasant, showed up. Don realised right away that he really didn't want to give up his fox. The reason he was doing so was that he expected to be leaving home in a week or so's time to work some distance away. He wouldn't be able to look after the fox, and his aunt couldn't do it. The only thing was to give it to someone who would promise to take care of it. He was talking about it as if it were a dog, Catherine thought. He wasn't selling it, though Don offered to pay him what-ever he'd given for it, or a bit more. But Ian Mackenzie didn't want any money. He wanted to be sure his fox would be happy, that was all. It was a vixen, he told Don. It had soon become used to people, because he took it with him when he went off to work in the forest. In the lorry with his work-mates it sat between his knees. It was on a collar and lead, and would wait quietly while he worked. He gave it some food during the day, and when he got it home in the evening it went into its home-made kennel and ate its

15

evening meal. Then young Mackenzie usually took it for a walk and it met the local dogs and became friendly with them. Again, Catherine thought, he makes it sound just like a dog.

Don learned how Ian Mackenzie had been given the fox. A man he knew and a gamekeeper had wiped out this fox-den up in the forest, but for one cub who'd escaped. The man had kept it for him. Catherine stayed chatting to Mrs Mackenzie, who prepared some tea, while Don went with the nephew to the yard where the fox was kept. Don noted how clean the home-made kennel was. The fox looked a wee bit reluctant to show itself when it saw him, but Ian Mackenzie took it up in his arms. It was in good condition, its coat well-brushed. It had lost its woolly blue and brown fur; it was quite rangey-looking, and hadn't yet got the darker muzzle of the fully-grown adult. Don realised how extraordinarily tame it was.

Young Mackenzie carried it to the Dormobile and Don got in and tied it by its lead to a seat-leg behind the driving-seat. It was wearing the dog-collar, which Don didn't like the idea of at all, but he didn't say anything. As a precaution in case the fox was car-sick he spread some polythene on the caravan floor.

Catherine got in, carefully eyeing the fox which in turn watched Ian Mackenzie all the time. He gave it a farewell pat, then stood by his aunt. Don fancied he was having a job not to cry, he was that much upset, saying good-bye to this fox that he'd cared for and tamed. Don drove off and glancing back saw young Mackenzie turn away quickly and go into the house. He didn't look back.

The fox sat gazing at Catherine. Its expression was gentle, quite unafraid. Don took the eastward road for Glencoe, into the Glen, wild and savage, and suddenly the fox stood on its hind legs, its front paws on the back of the driving-seat, as if wanting to see where it was going. Catherine put out a hand gingerly to pat it on the head. Its ears went down, but it wasn't meaning it in an aggressive manner. It was just feeling timid, meeting complete strangers. Catherine thought it extraordinary that it was so tame.

They drove through Rannoch Moor, strange and desolate, where, Don reminded his wife, young David Balfour and Alan Breck escaped their pursuers in Robert Louis Stevenson's *Kidnapped*. It made a dark, foreboding scene in the fading sunlight, and Catherine felt happier when they took the short cut through Glen Orchy's beautiful heather-covered slopes, one of her husband's favourite spots. Then on to Dalmally, the road back to Loch Awe, and home. The fox jumped up and down with its paws on the driving-seat several times, and Don could hear it slither about on the nylon. He glanced back every now and then to make sure it wasn't coming to any harm.

The road to Inverinan became narrow and winding again and as they came in sight of the village the fox was sick. Don felt duly thankful for the polythene.

It was half-past eight, and would be dark soon. Don wanted to give the fox the run of the enclosure before night fell, so that it would get to know its new home right away. He saw Meg Allan by the gate to his house and called out to her as he got down from the wheel. He went round to the caravan door as Catherine got out. The fox stood there, looking a little pathetic, and Don picked it up. As he did so he saw unmistakably that it was no vixen. It was a dog-fox. He wondered how Ian Mackenzie could have made such a mistake. It must have been because it had been so gentle. Don held the fox in his arms. It lay there, perfectly calm. The musky smell of its fur wasn't so very strong.

Meg was staring, hardly able to speak, so full of wonder was she at the sight of this fox, tame and gentle, in Don's arms. "What's its name?" she said.

"Rufus," Don replied on the spur of the moment.

Meg said the name to herself. She stroked his head gently. Rufus raised his jaw so that she could scratch him. He was obviously used to being stroked and patted. Meg saw how round the fox's eyes were. Not a bit sly or slanted as

she had expected them to be, but trusting and innocent. Catherine hurried into the house to prepare supper, while Don, Rufus in his arms, went to the garden. Meg followed him, longing to hold Rufus, but not daring to ask if she might. Perhaps later on, she thought.

Don had about an acre of garden, and he had enclosed one corner, sixty feet by fifteen feet, with a high wire-netting fence. Roofed with similar netting it took in a small tree. He had build a den, warm and waterproof, and banked it round with earth and small rocks to give it a natural appearance; but the roof could be lifted up to enable him to look into the den. It had two entrances—he knew that a fox liked to be able to come in one way and exit by another if it wanted to. The den really looked as natural as he could possibly make it.

Meg opened the gate of the enclosure, and Don put Rufus down. He removed the collar and lead. There was the mark round the neck where the collar had been, which Don hoped wouldn't remain there long. Rufus suddenly felt free of the collar and leapt into the air, as if with delight. Then he raced from end to end of the enclosure, searching each corner. It was beginning to get darker, but there was enough light for him to see where he was; and as Don and Meg watched him he paused by the den. Then, down into the tunnel, and after a few moments out again from the other tunnel. "It's all right, now," Don told Meg. "He knows exactly where he is." He knew that Rufus would use the den as his home. He would go into it at night if he wanted to, or shelter there if it rained.

From the garden the shore of Loch Awe was about three hundred yards away. Rufus had only to stand on top of his den and he could glimpse the gleaming water; beyond it the twin peaks of Ben Cruachen. A wonderful view.

While Meg stood watching him taking the measure of his new territory, Don fetched his food. It was a dish with meat and dog-biscuits in it. He opened the enclosure-gate again and put down the food. Immediately Rufus came over and began to eat. And once he did that—getting a young animal to eat when it's settling down in strange surroundings is sometimes difficult— Don knew all would be well. Better leave him now, he said, and went to the house. He looked back and saw the girl's shadowy figure still at the gate of the enclosure.

After supper, Don went out again with a torch, just to make sure that Rufus was all right. Meg had gone home. It was a warmish night, and it was dry. Rufus hadn't gone into his den. Don had fixed up a wooden bench just beside the den; he knew that often a fox prefers to lie on something above ground level, the branch of a tree, for instance, and he was glad to see Rufus on the bench, his brush curved round him in front on his face. He peered over it at Don, shadowed behind the torch.

"Goodnight, Rufus . . ." As he turned away, Don caught the answering flicker of the bushy tail. He went into the house to tell Catherine how happy he was about Rufus.

RUFUS, DON & MEG
CHAPTER TWO

DON MACCASKILL had been brought up to believe that foxes were pests which needed to be ruthlessly exterminated. You don't think about it when you're a boy, hearing the talk of shepherds and gamekeepers, you just believe what they tell you. You accept the stories of how foxes go about doing little else but killing lambs and game, and all the poultry they can find. This picture of a fox as a sly, skulking menace was built up in the mind from the time you first went out into the forest, or on to the hills. Poison, gassing, traps, hunting them down with dogs, nothing was too bad for the murderous fox. They had to be destroyed, every fox-den's occupant pitilessly obliterated.

During his first job as a forester near Glasgow Don encountered the same hatred of foxes on all sides; but he was starting to question the validity of this condemnation, voiced with such implacable detestation. It was a small forest on top of a hill, and the surrounding neighbourhood comprised small-holdings and poultry-farms. It wasn't sheep-farming country. Foxes used the forest as a hide-out during daylight, going down to the farms at night to get their food. There were few rabbits in the forest.

Apart from poultry farmers, another danger to the fox were sportsmen who organised fox-drives at regular intervals. Late one morning they had driven a particular part of the forest and as a result several victims of their guns lay beside them while they tucked into lunch.

Don still visualises the scene as he came upon it. The men sitting around with sandwiches and flasks of coffee and whisky—and this burly farmer in breeches and leggings, joking and deliberately emptying his gun-barrel at a fox already dead at his feet. "Take that, you bastard . . ."

Sick to his stomach at what he felt was something shameful, Don there and then vowed that once he was in charge of the forest there would never be any more fox-drives allowed. He determined to learn something about foxes and satisfy his scepticism regarding the crimes attributed to them. No God's creature, he felt sure, was so evil it deserved the desecration he had witnessed meted out to the dead fox.

He saw that the evidence of the fox's depredations was far from conclusive. To those who described to him how their poultry had been slaughtered by this notorious assassin of the night he would ask: How do you know it was a fox? Did you actually see it on the job? No, of course not, was the invariable reply, the injured party being in bed at the time. But there was the hen-house full of feathers, and half the birds missing. If you didn't see it, then it might have been a dog? No, it was a fox all right. Was the poultry-run securely locked up for the night? Well, no, I forgot about it, as it happens, and left the door open. In that case—even if it was a fox—it was your fault; you can't blame it for taking advantage of your mistake, a fox has to kill to eat, the same as most animals—and human beings. That's why there are so few rabbits in the forest, because rabbits are foxes' favourite food. So are rats and mice—that's what brings foxes down from the forest, not your poultry, but the rats and mice that infest the farms around. If you took care to keep your hen-house locked up at night, the foxes couldn't get at them. They'd get on with killing the rats and mice.

Of course, they wouldn't listen. It was ingrained in them. All their lives they had been taught that foxes were vermin that must be destroyed. Don was taken for the soft-hearted sort, a bit of a crank. He began looking out for foxes, observing where they made their dens, the rabbit-burrows they would take over. Sometimes he managed to catch sight of cubs at play, but this wasn't often. The great difficulty about trying to study the fox is that it is a nocturnal creature, staying hidden during the day.

It didn't occur to him that a good way to learn about foxes would be to keep one himself. Not at that time—he wouldn't have been able to keep one, anyway. To begin with he didn't have the right sort of space, and even if he had the uproar from his fox-hating neighbours would have been worse than if they'd discovered he was harbouring a criminal. All he could do to try and learn about foxes was to keep his eyes open. He read whatever magazine-articles and books he could lay his hands on. But there wasn't enough. Everything he read, and the shepherds and farmers he listened to, failed to come up with convincing reasons for destroying foxes. What they offered seemed to Don to be more emotive than logical.

Then Don and his family moved to Loch Aweside forest, to a house with a fair-sized garden. He started to plan in his mind an enclosure he might build where a fox would have reasonable freedom, where it could feel secure. Meanwhile he constructed a hide in the forest. He had become a useful photographer and built up quite a photo-library of birds and animals in the wild. The only animal he hadn't managed to photograph was the fox. Foxes were difficult. At night when they're usually on the move you can't see them for the dark, and by day they sleep holed up, or stay-put in their den.

But early in 1968, when he knew the vixen gives birth to her cubs, Don tried to find a den he could keep under observation. He had learned that you couldn't rely on a fox returning to the same spot where you'd last seen him holed up. Next day he'd have moved to some other place of cover. But during breeding-time the vixen lived in the den with her cubs, the dog-fox bringing food for them. That was his job. The trouble was that when Don tried to foresee what den a vixen would choose she wouldn't make up her mind. First it would be this rabbit-burrow, then she'd shift somewhere else. And move elsewhere again. Finally, he built his hide in a strategically-placed tree, on a ridge in the forest which overlooked the den where he'd calculated the vixen had at last decided upon. It was in a tiny valley, below a great slab of rock.

You must make your hide as inconspicuous as you can, with branches and heather, the roof waterproof to keep out the draught, and openings in front and at the sides through which you can see and push your camera. And you need something to sit on. It's a long vigil, waiting for a wild creature to show itself. And none will try your patience longer than the fox.

Foxes, Don had noticed, seldom look up, and as he concluded that those in which he was especially interested would approach their den from the valley he was less likely from his position in the tree on the ridge above to attract their notice. Also the wind would carry his scent high over them. He felt he might congratulate himself that his presence would remain undetected.

When you're dealing with foxes, however, you're dealing with the unpredictable. The first occasion he got up to the hide and prepared himself for a long wait—it was late afternoon with twilight an hour away—he heard the bark of a fox, *behind him*. It was the dog-fox, but for some reason he was approaching the den not up to it by way of the valley but down from the ridge above. He had got Don's scent, foxes are gifted with an almost supernatural scenting apparatus, and he was barking a warning to the vixen in the den.

Don climbed down from his hide and went home in the gathering dusk. It was bad luck, but he didn't give in. He returned next afternoon to discover what had been the effect of the dog-fox's warning bark on the vixen. Don thought it was reasonably certain that she had her litter of cubs in the den. Had she and her mate decamped with the cubs? He gained the den, not from the position of the hide, but a different direction, from behind a screen of trees to the side of it. He inched forward as quietly as he could. He was still hidden by the trees when suddenly there came a bark again. It was in the distance; this time it was the vixen who had picked up his scent, or she had heard him—her ears would be as sharp as her nose—and he guessed she was barking to warn the cubs down in the earth. So they were there, she hadn't shifted them, yet.

But she would now, Don was certain of it. Both she and her mate knew that their den had been discovered; instinctively they would have to move, taking the cubs with them. He came back the following day and sure enough there was no sign nor sound of them. They had stolen away in the night.

Added to his feeling of defeat at what had happened was the fact that the pair of foxes he had located were comparatively rare in the district. Loch Aweside is Highland country, sheep-farming country, preserved by gamekeepers who shot at sight anything that moved which might be reckoned to endanger the sheep. What with them and the shepherds the prospects for a fox surviving for long was grim.

Don set to work actively in his garden constructing a den and enclosure for a fox he could study and come to know. Then one day came the telephone-call from Mrs Mackenzie and the fulfilment of his hope and dream.

HE knew from the start that his first objective must be to gain Rufus's complete confidence. He hadn't been deceived by the fox's friendliness on the way from Ballachulish. He was on the lead then, under a certain amount of restraint. He couldn't get away, and he knew it. That was why Don hadn't liked it when he'd seen the collar and lead; he knew that was the way he had been brought up, except when he was shut away for the night in the kennel. It was a miserable life he wouldn't wish on a dog, let alone a wild thing like a fox. He didn't blame Ian Mackenzie, he couldn't be expected to know any better. He'd kept his pet in good physical condition, but he couldn't read a fox's mind, comprehend how he was reacting mentally to the continued curtailment of his freedom, for which every instinct in him longed. Don remembered the way Rufus had leapt into the air when his collar had been removed as he was put into the enclosure. It was the first chance he had been given to jump and leap about like that in the whole of his life. You could see in every line of his dancing body how he had exulted in it, his joyousness as he raced round the enclosure, revelling in the free space.

Inevitably, the moment he no longer felt the collar round his neck, the tugging lead holding him back, he reverted to some extent to a wilder state. When Don was to explain this to Meg, she understood. She also recalled how Rufus had sought out the bounds of his territory, how he had made for the den, instinctively finding that there was another tunnel to it by which he could exit or enter.

Don would need to give as much time as he could to Rufus if they were going to become friends. Patience and time. Time to talk quietly to him, appear relaxed, move unhurriedly, and sit down. Patience, so that you never made any attempt to approach him, just sat and waited for him to come to you. You didn't call or try to coax him, you mustn't encourage him. You just have to wait.

Don had a look at him the next morning on his way to work, just to make sure Rufus was all right after his journey and that he had food. He seemed to be slightly nervous. That evening, the second of Rufus's arrival, he'd had all day to settle down in his fresh surroundings, to feel secure and self-confident

in the new circumstances in which he found himself. Don wanted him to learn it all for himself without anyone around keeping an eye on him. When he let himself in through the wire gate, Rufus still watched him nervously. He was offered food, but he didn't want it. Don considered him for a moment, then gave him a nod. "Good-night, Rufus . . ." He didn't glance back to see if there'd been that responsive flick of the brush. But he doubted it.

After that it was a visit twice a day, always relaxed and unhurried, with a few quiet words. Rufus was eating the food that was given him when he was alone; he looked well and alert. But it took him a week before he made up his mind and moved towards Don very watchfully. Don kept still, trying to appear as unconcerned as he could, when Rufus began to come to him. Very slowly. He allowed Don to pat him on the head, before he backed away and moved off. Don felt that his patience was going to repay him.

The next evening Meg Allan called. Don had already gone to the enclosure, and she caught up with him as he was going in. She had called every afternoon to inquire after Rufus and to spend some time watching him from outside the enclosure. She would talk to him very quietly, not attempting to encourage him into coming to her—Don had explained to her that it was best to let him do so of his own accord. She would stand there for long minutes of sheer enchantment, without stirring, and he would stare back at her with his round, innocent eyes. Then he would turn to lope gracefully off, brush held low and balancing him as with a swift movement he looked back at her and then moved away again. After a while she would call good-bye quietly, and he would always turn his head to stare at her. Sometimes she would receive the impression that he was about to make a move towards her. But he remained where he was. She would turn to see him as she went round the corner of the house. He always watched her out of sight.

This evening Rufus was by his den, apparently absorbed in contemplating several sparrows on the wire-netting roof. She was about to say that she would come back another time; she knew that Don preferred to be by himself while he was making friends with Rufus. But he told her to come into the enclosure. He said quietly how Rufus had come to him the previous evening and permitted himself to be patted on the head. She let herself in, moving slowly, to join Don. The sparrows flew away, and as if their flight now gave him an opportunity to give Meg his undivided attention—of course, the had been aware of her arrival all the time—Rufus turned to her.

Don was perfectly still, and Meg had followed his example. He had told her how you would never alarm Rufus by remaining absolutely still, without a movement. It would be bound to arouse his curiosity, which sooner or later would almost certainly overcome his suspicion. Rufus concentrated his attention upon her, head slightly on one side, round eyes inquiring. It was a long scrutiny. She kept quiet as a statue, and then his attitude relaxed; still staring at her, he gave a sudden leap into the air, as if pouncing upon something. Don said to Meg in an undertone that he was pretending to hunt a mouse. Rufus gave a couple more leaps, still without taking his eyes off Meg, pouncing on his imaginary prey. She was careful not to laugh or move, and he stopped and carried out a series of leaps, looking at her all the time. It was almost as if he were inviting her to join in with him in some sort of game.

Don was smiling to himself, but Meg remained serious-faced. She was filled with an indescribable emotion of affection, the warmth of her love for Rufus made her long to hold him close. But she stayed still. Rufus had sat down, evidently puzzled by his failure to make any impression upon her. Don knew that at any moment now he would make a move towards her. With a word to her, he went slowly out of the enclosure. He pretended to take an interest in the garden, while keeping an eye on Rufus, waiting for him to make a move to Meg. She made as if about to follow Don, then turned and waited. Rufus hesitated, then came to her, slowly, and allowed her to put her hand on his head.

Meg stayed with him for several minutes, talking to him quietly, feeling the warm softness of his fur. She put her face against his, smelling his warm, musky scent. Don watched them, he knew there wasn't any danger of Rufus biting her, until presently it was time for Meg to go home. When she had gone, Don went back into the enclosure. The shadows were stealing across the garden; over in the direction of Loch Awe a solitary star glimmered. It was about half-an-hour after Meg had gone that Rufus came over to Don and let him pat his head. Then he jumped away, came back again and lay down, his bushy tail curved in front of his nose, while Don sat and talked to him. He stood up and went quietly out. "Goodnight, Rufus . . ." He sensed rather than saw an answering flick from the brush.

RUFUS IN THE LIMELIGHT
CHAPTER THREE

WORD got round that there was a tame fox in Don MacCaskill's garden. Meg was telling her school-friends all about Rufus and asked permission to bring them to see him. Don was only too pleased to encourage children to show an interest in wild life; he was all for them, and also their parents, visiting the forest, enjoying its beauty and the sight of a variety of birds and animals: badgers, red squirrels and deer. Rufus, after appearing somewhat wary at first, quickly took to the children—the fact that Meg was with them was to him sufficient guarantee of their friendliness. She instructed them to behave calmly and control their exceitement when they saw this fox at close quarters. He would run to meet them, stand on his hind-legs, fore-paws against the enclosure fence, wagging his wonderful tail and, eyes shut in blissful innocence, allow the more adventurous of the children to push their fingers through the wire-netting in order to scratch his white chest.

Soon they were sharing their sweets with him. A grocer's motor-van came round every day and stopped outside Don's house; Meg and her friends bought a coconut-and-cream concoction called "Snowballs" which proved a great favourite with Rufus. The children would club together to buy him not one "Snowball", but more. And more. He could tuck away half-a-dozen at a time with no difficulty at all, and what was so marvellous was his way of eating them so that they left a big white moustache across his face, a much more bizarre effect than anything his delighted audience ever managed to achieve.

Don realised how deep Meg's attachment to Rufus had become. She was allowed into the enclosure whenever she wished; she was always careful to obtain permission first and spent most of her spare time with Rufus, playing games with him or holding him in her arms and talking to him. She found an old tennis-ball which she would throw in the air and he would chase after; he would allow it to roll still, pretend to turn away and then with a show of elaborate nonchalance give his sidelong leap to pounce on it. It was his hunting-the-mouse performance, and he would oblige with as many encores as requested. Then there was a hide-and-seek game: Rufus would dive into his den and Meg must guess which of the two tunnels he would exit from, and try to catch him as he did so. She never succeeded, he always knew at which exit she was waiting for him and would shoot out of the other, his brush flickering to keep him balanced as he twisted and turned at top speed. But Meg took care never to startle him with an unexpected, sudden movement when they weren't playing. She spoke to him quietly and always waited for him to come to her, never chased after him when he was disposed to be on his own.

Don and his wife had thought of Meg as shy and reserved, younger than her years. It appeared that she wasn't especially outstanding at her lessons, except natural history and essay-writing. She had confided in Catherine that

she loved writing poetry and had written several poems about Rufus—but she hadn't told anyone else about it. Don had a passing acquaintance with her father. He was a big man, handsome-looking, who always wore an open-necked shirt, winter and summer. He had his daughter's soft voice, even something of her gentle manner, though like his father before him who had been gamekeeper on the same estate, he was reputed to be a crack shot; and none came wiser in the ways of the deer and game on the hills and moors round about than Joe Allan.

Meg had got to know Don when he had visited the school, as he did several times a year, to talk about wild-life and show his photographs. She had stood up and asked questions, she wanted to know more about foxes especially; what he had said concerning them had caught her imagination. Later, she had

called at his house, cradling a baby red squirrel with an injured foot which she had found. She hadn't liked taking it home, she admitted; she was afraid she would be told that the best way to cure the little squirrel was to kill it. She had asked more about foxes; her father always reviled them, never a good word to say for foxes. She supposed, she said, that was why she had begun to feel a kind of sympathy for them. Because they were so hated by everyone. It was difficult to believe, she thought, that God could have created such a "cruel, detestable creature" as the fox was supposed to be, though she never let her father know what she had come to believe.

The main reason, Don said, why people had it in for foxes was because the Highlands was sheep country; ever since sheep had been introduced a hundred and fifty years ago the fox had been branded a killer. The fact that the fox was there centuries before and that his home, the forest, where he had lived on his staple diet of mice and rabbits, had been cut down to give sheep grazing space, was never taken into account. Of course, the fox was a natural predator, and if he couldn't get rabbits he went for what other food he could find. In fact, lambs were available for only a couple of months in the year and a fully-grown sheep was too formidable for a fox to tackle, so that left him the remaining ten months in which he had to provide for himself. Hundreds of sheep die yearly, and it was these that provided foxes with a certain amount of food. As for Meg's father, well, he was a gamekeeper, and it was his job, of course, to protect the grouse which had been the fox's natural food in the forest. Now, thousands of grouse were bred artificially for sportsmen to shoot, but the fox was abominated for wanting a few for himself. Even so, he killed many more rats than he ever did grouse, and rats were notorious for destroying grouse-eggs and the chicks.

Always these stories were against the fox, myths that had been spread out of ignorance and fear; practically nothing was known of the fox's life-history —except that it was a nocturnal creature, and human beings were still afraid of the dark; night-time was still thought of by some as the time of evil spirits and baleful monsters bent on harm and destruction. The vilest, most murderous cunning was attributed to foxes, which in fact they possessed no more than other wild animals. If they were all that cunning, Don pointed out, why was it that their dens are so easy to find, not hidden secretly away? You always knew where a fox's earth was by the bits and pieces of feather and bone, remains of food brought to the den—deliberately left outside for the cubs to play with, and with which the vixen taught them how to hunt. It was more their lack of cunning and stealth which brought about their destruction; it

was because they continued to make a life without instinctively covering up their tracks that they were relatively easy to hunt down.

Meg saw the sense in what Don had been saying; all the same he didn't want her blurting out a lot of notions to her father which to him must sound like blasphemy. He was careful to point out to her that with some, hating foxes was like a religion. You'd be banging your head against a brick wall to try to get them to change the beliefs of a life-time overnight. If ever. It only made for bad feeling to try. You just had to hang on to what you believed to be true, despite all prejudice, and wait for a chance to speak out when you thought it would do most good. Meg agreed; she was much too scared of how her father might react if he learned that she had any such ideas in her head, even though he had smiled indulgently at her interest in this tame fox of Don MacCaskill.

She would write an essay on it, she told Don, for her next natural history lesson. As well as her secret poems, she had already written essays about wildlife in school. Her teacher had even asked her if she'd thought of studying to become a veterinary surgeon, but Meg didn't believe she'd be clever enough to pass the exams; and anyway her parents couldn't afford to pay for the training even if she did.

As well as Rufus proving such a magnet for the village children, those from outlying places got to know about him, and they and their parents driving through Inverinan would stop at the house to ask if it was true that a marvellously tame fox lived here. Some brought their cameras, and Don was always willing to persuade Rufus to pose for his picture. Unlike most animals, he was only too pleased and quickly up on his hindlegs, front-paws stretched up against the fence to show off his chest, wagging his fine tail, white teeth glistening in a wide grin of joy. One week-end the visitors included a family from Edinburgh, father, mother, son and daughter. They had heard about Rufus, and the amount of the father's photographic gear showed how seriously he took his hobby. Rufus posed with his usual eagerness, but the man, not altogether satisfied with what he'd got, asked if he might take some photographs from inside the enclosure. The wire-netting was getting in the way, he explained. Don thought this might scare Rufus off, but then decided that it couldn't cause any harm and allowed the photographer inside.

Where Don had expected that Rufus might now follow the usual pattern of animals and back away, he immediately came up and pushed his nose right into the lens as the man tried to get him in focus, so that it was the photographer who found himself backing away. And then when at last he was about to click his camera Rufus dodged behind him and was dashing off with his exposure-meter, depositing it in his den, before nipping back for a further item of equipment.

Watching him go through his endearing antics, it was brought home to Don how individual Rufus had become; he had developed a personality of his own, seemingly having learned to play games for fun, for his own and others' amusement. You could say that he possessed a sense of humour, and if that was too much to believe at least he had learned a game that had nothing to do with animal instinct.

Sometimes, to the delight of the children who would crowd round, Don would carry him in his arms. He didn't seem to mind how much his brush was pulled or he was scratched under his chin, or his ears tweaked, everyone marvelling how tame he was; why, you could hardly believe he was really a fox at all.

ESCAPE
CHAPTER FOUR

WINTER, 1968, and the first fall of snow.

Rufus came out of his den slowly, contemplating the snow with wonder. It was the first time he had seen it, and his usually round eyes narrowed questioningly. He tried to recognise his surroundings which had changed so drastically overnight, for when he had gone to sleep the world had been varying shades from grey to black. Now, everywhere another colour had appeared. White. Sparkling, shimmering white. And feathery flakes that fell endlessly to settle at his feet without so much sound as a sigh. He glanced back at the imprints of his footsteps in the snow; as he trotted on they trotted after him. He jumped up to snap the flakes between his teeth, but they were only an icy, wet sensation on his tongue. He could feel a clinging whiteness about his face, above his eyes. He shook himself, and powdered snow sprayed off his shoulders. For a moment his expression was startled. He decided it was nothing to worry about, and exhilaration filled him as he raced round in a shower of white.

He made a fine handsome fox, his biggish bones well covered, flanks filling out; his brush was magnificently full and the snow showed off his winter coat.

Three weeks after Christmas the snow had cleared and milder weather set in. Don was in his office when at midday a passing lorry-driver pulled up outside and put his head round the door. On his way to work he had seen a fox. "Whereabouts was that?" About a mile up the road, and the driver gave a description of the fox. Tried to run it down, he had. But it had just trotted on ahead. He had tried to catch up with it, but then it had turned into a quarry half-a-mile away. He had been so determined to kill it that he had turned into the quarry after it, but it had jumped on to a rock and sat and stared at him. He got out of his lorry, picking up a lump of rock and throwing it at the fox, but he missed, and it promptly ran into the forest.

The moment the lorry-driver had left this office Don hurried out to his car and drove quickly home. Something about the description of the fox and its manner made him anxious, and it so happened that he had left home that morning without looking in on Rufus as was his invariable habit. He had been delayed by trouble with his car and there had been some urgent matters waiting him at the office. As he stopped at his house and hurried into the garden he felt sick with apprehension. Sure enough, the enclosure-gate was open, and no Rufus.

He paused long enough to note that the gate was propped wide with a piece of stick; it had been opened deliberately, either late the previous night or early in the morning. Giving Catherine a shout, telling her what had happened, he drove off to the quarry where Rufus—it was he the lorry-driver had tried to run down without a doubt—had last been seen. But there was no sign of him. Don went into the forest, calling for him, but it was no use. He spent the rest of the day searching, but still no Rufus. He realised that he had probably been scared by the lorry-driver, never before had a hand been raised against him in anger, and he had probably decided to hide during the day; he wouldn't move during daylight, but would be lying up in the brushwood, from where he wouldn't come out for anyone, not even for Don.

Don returned home, disconsolate at the prospect that he would probably never see Rufus again. Meg and several of the children called round early in the evening and once they had got over the shock of Don's news immediately clamoured to make up a search-party. Meg, as she rushed out to the enclosure, to make sure that he hadn't somehow returned, could barely believe what had happened. The empty enclosure, no response to her call, "Rufus . . . Rufus . . ." Sickened at the thought that he would never be found, she hurried back to the house and set off with Don and the children.

There are extensive spruce woods with thick bracken in this area around the quarry and any hope of coming across Rufus was remote. Don had explained to Meg how he felt Rufus would have reacted to the lorry-driver's antagonism, and consequently would wait until nightfall before venturing out to search for food. Don, Meg and the children covered the area for a mile or more around, until it was supper-time and too dark to see. It was a sad, silent group who headed back to the village.

No news of Rufus the next day, or the next. Every day Don, Meg and various bands of children had set out on a new search first thing every morning before Don went to work, during lunch-time and again in the evening. But Rufus might have been spirited away. Don began to feel certain that either he was dead or had been so scared by the lorry-driver that he would never show his face to a human being again. Meg, however, had recovered some of her lost hope and now refused to believe that he wouldn't come back; each night she prayed for his safety and that he would return.

Two weeks after Rufus's escape Don was down by Loch Awe; he was on the look-out this time for a migrant osprey which had been reported near the loch. There aren't more than a score of these birds in the Highlands and Scottish isles and Don was anxious to check that it was indeed an osprey which had been seen.

He had parked his car near a lodge by the forest and made his way quietly to the loch-shore. He waited patiently, and after an hour without sighting the bird, he turned to go home. Reaching his car he saw something on the lodge-gate . A brownish-red object—a fox, he knew at once. Somebody must have killed it. The loch-side was over seven miles from

Inverinan, but Rufus could easily have travelled that distance. His heart turning to ice, Don went to the gate. The brush had been cut off—the brush is the trophy for which the reward paid is twenty shillings—but he saw that it was a vixen, and Don drove away. He knew that this was the fate that could easily be in store for Rufus, if in fact he had not already suffered it.

Don didn't mention the dead vixen to Meg that evening when she accompanied him on another vain search. She continued to hope, though the rest of the children had given up Rufus for lost. Next day passed with still no news; Don, with Meg, had scoured the area, up and down the roadside, searching the forest, places where Rufus might be expected to hunt for food. He wasn't really old enough to be able to take care of himself properly, he'd had no experience of hunting, but Don kept a look-out at any farm he passed, in case of any complaint of a missing hen which Rufus might have tried for. He heard none and concluded that if he were still alive Rufus was living off mice and rats. He doubted if he would go for a rabbit, since he had always behaved in his usual friendly manner towards any of the children's pet rabbits when they'd been introduced to him. He might even have treated any rat or mouse as a playmate.

By the week's end, Don had given up all hope, though Meg still felt that her prayers would be answered. It was late on Saturday afternoon when a mother of one of the Inverinan children who had earlier helped in the search, called at the house. She had seen a fox at the roadside, near a farm on the village outskirts, and from her description Don thought it might be Rufus. He drove to the place quickly. The farm had fairly extensive land round it, the house itself was surrounded by big trees and rhododendron-bushes. The sort of place Rufus might have chosen to lie up during the day, and Don set about turning the area over. Just as he emerged from the rhododendrons, suddenly there was Rufus, running aimlessly to and fro. Don called to him quietly. At once he paused, and without hesitation came straight to Don, his brush wagging, though his ears were laid back and his expression was apprehensive, as though expecting to receive a scolding for all the anxiety and trouble he had caused. Just like a dog, Don thought, speaking to him gently. Rufus crouched close, and Don made to pick him up, but as he did so Rufus turned and dodged away, tail still wagging, however. He wanted to be picked up and comforted, but was still fearful that he was in for punishment.

Don followed him to the edge of the rhododendron-bushes, talking to him quietly. He kept his voice down not only to reassure him but because he had heard the clucking of poultry nearby and feared that the farmer would come out to deal summarily with this fox that was about to attack his hens. Again Rufus crouched, and again he ran off when Don reached for him. This time, Don saw the poultry-run round the corner of the house. So did Rufus, who made straight for the hen-house entrance, where the fowls were settling down for the night. The aperture was invitingly open, the farmer hadn't yet closed it, and to Don's consternation Rufus went straight in.

The noise of wildly beating wings and hysterical cackling seemed to Don to be deafening. At any moment someone must appear from the farm. Don couldn't get into the hen-house to reach Rufus, it was locked. He didn't know what to do—and then Rufus reappeared, in his jaws an enormous, screeching hen, half its feathers missing. It was obvious that Rufus had no intention of killing it, to him it was just part of some new game, but it was doubtful if the farmer would believe it. Don made a dive and caught him by the tail. Rufus opened his mouth to protest at this unwarranted interruption of his playful antics, and let the hen go. Still squawking, but unharmed except for losing half its plumage, it shot back into the hen-house, from which feathers swirled out. Rufus was now in Don's arms fondly licking his face; there was to be **no** scolding. His ribs could be felt very plainly, and it was doubtful if he had enjoyed much to eat the past three weeks.

Don caught the sound of voices raised in inquiry from the direction of the farmhouse. He didn't wait to offer any explanations but clutched Rufus to him and hurried to his car. Rufus sat up beside him during the drive, gazing out with interest at the gathering dusk.

NEW FRIENDS
CHAPTER FIVE

T HE moon that early February night shone coldly; its metallic gleam turned the forest into an army of black motionless giants, even the topmost branches were still. Came the nearby "kee-wick" of a tawny owl above Don Mac-Caskill's head and he saw its ghostly wings with its round face drift noiselessly past. Don paused, and it was then that from the direction of the shore of the loch he heard the yap of the dog-fox. He stood still, and sure enough the screech of the vixen sounded in reply. He went towards his car, parked on the edge of the forest. He was on his way back home after spending near enough three hours trying to learn if the dog-fox was, in fact, in the vicinity. Not only was he there all right, but the vixen had joined him, which meant that unless she was disturbed she would make a home for herself and the cubs to which she would soon be giving birth.

As head forester, he had long done his best to ensure that no unauthorised person set foot in the forest to hunt foxes; but despite his efforts he was well aware that there were farmers, shepherds—or a rabbit poacher, out to pick up that twenty shillings reward—who would never give up their bitter feud, and if they knew that a fox was in the neighbourhood they would track it down and destroy it. Shoot, trap or gas—whatever means that could be most effectively employed. They were the sort who had deliberately let out Rufus, bent on killing him. How he had escaped destruction at the moment of his release, must have been miraculous; some intuition must have warned him and he'd managed to slip away into the darkness before he was caught.

Don reached his car by the roadside, full of doubt that the pair of foxes he'd just heard calling to each other would be allowed to live in peace. The vixen's cry had turned his thoughts to a nagging problem that had lain at the back of his mind since Rufus's return. Oh, he had settled down well enough, obviously delighted to be back once more with those who loved him. But Don realized that the time had come when Rufus would have to return to the wild.

It was there that he belonged, not in captivity. However free he was to

M. MAJOR

enjoy the company of Don and Meg, the children and the visitors who came to see him, the motive for obtaining him in the first place no longer held water. Rufus had become so tame that he could hardly be compared with a fox as it normally existed. He was no longer a wild creature to be studied at close quarters; he'd become a friend as well-loved as a domesticated dog or cat. On the surface at any rate. But Rufus was a wild creature, his present existence was entirely false; he was being denied his true right to live the life for which he had been born, the heritage to which he was entitled.

You couldn't begin to understand what were Rufus's real longings. He played games with Meg and the children, he went through his performances, posed for the photographers, revelling in the admiration and amusement he caused. You could easily imagine that his life was complete. He seemed so happy and content with his lot. And, of course, compared with what most other young foxes suffered, the gin-trap, or being gassed into extinction, he had nothing to complain about.

But this was from the human viewpoint; it wasn't possible to take into account what really went on behind that tapering head of his. What thoughts spun around in his mind at night, when he was alone, listening to the sounds all around him. He might even have heard a vixen's call as Don had. What instinctive emotions would he experience, emotions which no human being, no matter how loving, could understand because Rufus simply couldn't communicate these things to anyone except his own kind?

Even Meg, who was closer probably than Don to Rufus, realised what an enormous gulf separated her from him. Don had warned her never to forget that she was dealing with a fox and not a human being, and not to judge him by human standards. There were experiences she could never share with him. What Rufus saw, for example, was very different from what she saw when they looked at the same object. To her it was in colour, to him it was in monochrome, varying shades of grey; the view of the sunset behind the purpling hills and the evening star, which thrilled Meg, the sky at dawn over the loch—these meant little or nothing to Rufus. Compared with her, Rufus was short-sighted, but he could rely on his powers of scent and hearing to an extent that she could hardly comprehend. He lived in his own world. A world no human being could hope to enter, not even Meg or Don, however much they loved him.

But though Rufus couldn't speak his thoughts aloud to a human being, wouldn't he possess instincts which must conjure up images in his mind? Memories in the blood, instinctive recognition of circumstances or situations connected with his wild state which he had barely experienced before he had passed into the hands of Ian Mackenzie at Ballachulish. This was what Don faced as he tried to make up his mind what was really best for Rufus, who was, after all, not a domesticated pet but a wild fox. He discussed it, of course, many times over with Catherine but he had practically made up his mind to release Rufus in the coming autumn. Viewing the situation from Rufus's point of view, the autumn would be the natural time when the cub leaves his family, when he has learned all he can from his parents and is pushed out to fend for himself. So it would be appropriate then, September to October, for Rufus to leave his family, Don, Meg and the children, and go out on his own.

Putting what he knew to be right into practice wasn't going to be easy for him and, as he told Catherine, he preferred not to think about it at the moment but to make the most of the time he had left with Rufus. He didn't say anything to Meg about what he had decided. Time enough for that when it came.

SEVERAL weeks after Rufus's safe return Cassius came on the scene. He was a kitten who had been holed up under the floorboards of a derelict house on the outskirts of Inverinan, which was being demolished. A workman had called at Don's house one evening and told him of this kitten which, so he said, was the offspring of a wild-cat father with a domestic cat for its mother. There were wild cats in that part of the Highlands, they made their homes

high up in the rocky cairns, sometimes coming down to the village for food when it was scarce in the hills. Don knew that male wild cats had been known to mate with a female domestic cat and produce offspring.

He went along to the house and underneath the floorboards sure enough was the kitten. He managed to reach it with one hand, but it dodged out of his grasp and spat and acted like a wild cat. "A real Cassius Clay, that's what he is," the workman said. Which was how it came to get its name. Don found a length of wire and pushed it along under the floorboards. The kitten had retreated as far as it could go, and the idea of the wire was to put it through the kitten's fur, dragging it out bodily. This is, by the way, a good method of getting a fox-cub out of a hole; you simply push in the length of wire and turn it till it catches in the fur and then you can pull the cub out.

It was then that Don made a discovery. Under the same floorboards, only a few feet away, he found four other kittens and the mother. Obviously the one the workmen had found on its own had belonged to that litter, and Don returned it to the others and went back home. The matter didn't end there. Next evening, Don had been home from work about an hour when he heard a mewing in the shed outside the back door. All five kittens were in a dark corner, but no sign of the mother. For some reason she had decided that Don could look after the family while she went off on her own.

The kitten named Cassius had a typical wild-cat appearance, like a little tiger, with a tiger's mentality. Its tail wasn't as short as a wild cat's but that would be remedied later. Don and Catherine found homes for the other four kittens but kept Cassius, who had immediately attached himself to them. The next step was to introduce him to Rufus.

Normally, foxes are deadly antagonistic to all cats, however young, but Don felt confident that Rufus would be friendly towards Cassius, who, in any case, didn't wait to be introduced. The morning after his arrival he found his way to the enclosure and quickly climbed the wire-netting to the top, where he sat staring down at Rufus. Then he jumped down to rub his fur against the wire-netting as Rufus ran up to him. Rufus gave a sniff, then he, too, pushed himself along the fence, his fur rubbing against that of Cassius through the wire-netting.

Don didn't feel quite ready to allow the kitten into the enclosure with Rufus, but with the fence between them Cassius's first move every morning when he was let out of the house was straight to the enclosure. He and Rufus would go through the routine of rubbing themselves against each other through the wire-netting and Cassius would then climb up on to the roof and

48

spend an hour or so observing Rufus down below.

The following week Don and Meg were in the garden with Rufus, playing his game of pouncing on the old tennis-ball, when Catherine called to Don to come into the house. He hurried in without mentioning to Meg about keeping Rufus with her. On this occasion, however, Rufus ran after Don and, despite Meg telling him to come back, followed him into the sitting-room. Cassius was lying on the hearth before the fire. Rufus took in the scene and promptly stretched himself out, side by side with Cassius. You would have thought he was a dog that had come in after a tiring run out-of-doors. From that time on Rufus was often invited—or invited himself—into the house to spend an hour with Cassius on the hearth-rug. They might have been the oldest of friends.

Cassius had no fear of any living thing—man or animal—which was to get him into trouble before long. He was outside the gate leading to the house when he was attacked by a passing dog. Cassius was prepared to give battle, then realised that he wasn't going to get away with it. He had to turn and run. Before he had reached the first branch of a nearby tree the dog leapt and nipped his tail and broke the end off it. Cassius stayed away from home two days and Don and Catherine thought he was lost. On the third day he turned up again, but the end of his tail was still bleeding. It was about this time that Don had got to know David Stephen, the noted Scottish naturalist who is especially interested in foxes. He was able to perform a veterinary surgeon's job on what remained of the tail and it healed. Cassius now sported a very short-ringed tail which together with his tiger stripes gave him the appearance of a real wild cat, apart from a white chest and white feet that betrayed his maternal origins.

His first action after David Stephen had attended to his tail was to look up Rufus and bring him back to the house, where they stretched out together before the sitting-room fire. Soon there was to be a third member of the party.

Two years before, while Catherine and Don were on their summer holiday, their seventeen-year-old Labrador dog had died, and had it not been for the arrival of Rufus, Don and Catherine would have owned another dog. Now, a Labrador puppy, a bitch, was offered to them by a friend on the other side of Inverinan. Don was anxious to have it mainly for Catherine's sake. Rufus was pretty well monopolised by Don himself and Meg, and since his wife was indoors so much anyhow she didn't get many opportunities to be with him. Shuna, as the puppy was named, would take the place of their old

Labrador who'd been a real home-loving dog. From the moment she arrived however, she immediately took to Rufus, and he as readily to her. He was, if anything, more friendly towards her than she to him. She was just a bit frightened by his strange smell. It wasn't a dog smell, it was a musky, fox's smell. But within several minutes they were playing together happily.

Rufus, following his practice at Ballachulish, had already made friends with the dogs in the village, and from the start Shuna was in the enclosure with him, or in the garden or bringing him to the house to share the hearth-rug with Cassius. The three of them played together. Don and Meg at first stood by looking on to see that the newcomer would meet no harm, and also that Rufus didn't take the opportunity to slip away. But there seemed to be no danger of this; the only problem was getting hold of Rufus when it was time for him to return to his enclosure on his own. But Shuna came in helpful here. One part of a game they played was for Rufus to lie on his back while Shuna nosed him over. When Don wanted Rufus in the enclosure again he would instruct Shuna, when Rufus was on his back, to hold him down with her paw on his stomach. Don would come along and pick up Rufus, carrying him off to be safely secured in his wire-netting home for the night. They made a wonderful trio, Rufus, nocturnal creature though he was, had yet accommodated himself in order to be with Don and Meg, and now with Shuna and Cassius, to becoming a day-time animal. He spent as much time awake during the daylight hours as he would have spent asleep had he been living in the wild.

CRONK
CHAPTER SIX

SHORTLY after Shuna joined the family, Don was in the forest near the rock-slab below the ridge where he had built the hide from which to observe the pair of foxes he had frightened away. At the time he had noticed a raven's nest on a ledge of this rock formation. Now, as he stood underneath the rock, he remembered the raven's nest, and wondered if it was still there. He saw that it was and at the same time there was a rush of wings as a raven flew off. Something fell, a dark shape which tumbled slowly down. He got to it to find a young raven lying on the ground. It appeared uninjured except that some of its claws had been pulled off as it tried to grasp at branches and jutting rock on its way down.

He made attempts to return the young bird to its nest, but it was in too inaccessible a place. He pulled off his jersey and wrapped the raven in it. About three weeks old, he thought it would be, with its enormous bill completely out of proportion to its body, and its wicked-looking, gleaming eyes. He took it home and improvised a cage out of a box, in the bottom of which he built a simple nest of sticks bound with wool. He put the young raven into the nest and got some food for it. You have to force-feed a young bird to begin with, it won't take food from anyone other than its mother—regurgitated food which she pushes down the youngster's throat. Don used a spoon to shovel down the food and the chick took it without any trouble; after that he and Catherine fed it every two hours for the next three days and nights.

The raven grew, squawked and attracted Cassius who had to investigate. Shuna came along; Don and Meg watched while Rufus, Cassius and Shuna gave this black object in the cage the once-over. Cassius sniffed at it—there is a strong odour about all the crow family, to which the raven belongs, and Cassius at first didn't like it and came away quickly. It's a rank smell, which the birds retain even into adulthood. It's not particularly pleasant, but you get used to it. Rufus appeared interested, so did Shuna; they together with Cassius, though he was still the least enthusiastic, visited the raven in its cage daily, as if to note its progress.

In fact, it made good progress, growing rapidly, and Don gave it the name of Cronk because of the squawking noise it made. *Cronk . . . Cronk . . .* Don had no intention of taming it, merely to rear it until it could fly, when he would release it. While it was in the nest Don acted as if he was its mother, feeding it with pieces of meat, but once it left the nest and started perching on the piece of branch which Don arranged it was feeding itself. He took it to a veterinary surgeon to deal with the claws torn out during its fall down the cliff. An injection, and the swelling caused by the injury healed, and at the same time it was discovered that Cronk was, in fact, a female.

By the sixth week Cronk was ready to fly. She had been flapping her wings while she was inside the cage, much to the interest of Rufus, Shuna and Cassius, and Don decided it was time to let her go. Though he hadn't consciously tried to tame Cronk, by feeding her he had, as he realised, imprinted himself on her so that she thought he was her mother.

Don took Cronk, flapping her wings excitedly, out of the cage and went into the garden. "Goodbye, Cronk . . ." and threw her into the air. Of course, Rufus was there, with Meg, and Shuna and Cassius, to see what happened.

What happened was that Cronk flew upwards strongly, but after a few

moments she dived down again and landed on Don's shoulder. He took her and, once again, threw her into the air. This time she flew round the garden and landed on the top of Rufus's enclosure. Rufus hurried into the enclosure, climbed up the tree and examined Cronk more closely. Cronk promptly bent down and stuck her beak through the wire-netting to give Rufus a friendly peck, but he ignored it. By this time Don had reached Cronk and took her off the enclosure-roof and put her down in the garden. She didn't fly off, but strutted around just like some sort of black parrot, *Cronk . . . Cronk . . .* Shuna very gingerly went up to her and stretched out her nose to give her a sniff. Cronk put her big, curved beak to Shuna's nose and gave her a little nip, quite gently, a warning to her not to take any liberties. Shuna retreated and sat down to ruminate over this black, strutting creature. Cassius went over to Shuna and sat next to her as if to reassure her that this new addition to the family was going to be a friend. Provided, that was, you watched her beak.

Rufus's real introduction to Cronk was when he was in the garden playing with Cassius and Shuna with the inevitable old tennis ball. Cronk flew down and landed on Rufus's back and tried to tweak one of his ears. Rufus, for all that he was so tame, thought this was taking a bit of a liberty. After all, he hadn't been properly introduced to Cronk. He promptly shook her off his back and chased after her. She made no attempt to fly away but faced up to him, but Rufus moved in fast. Adroitly he caught her by the neck and gave her a jolly good shaking. Meg, who was watching with Don, caught her breath. And Don was suddenly afraid that Rufus would revert to type, so to speak, and bite Cronk. But you didn't have to worry about old Rufus. Cronk was perfectly all right, and from that moment she and Rufus became close friends. Cronk never attempted to peck Rufus again, she knew her place all right when it came to dealing with so formidable a character as she realised the fox could be.

Neither did Cronk attempt to peck Don. Even Meg, or Catherine or the other children, were liable to receive a nip from her if she felt in a paricular mood, but Don could rub his face against hers and she would coo and jabber away to him happily, fluttering her wings as if asking him to feed her. To her he was still her mother.

The raven is not really a black-coloured bird, though it looks black. It has many colours in its feathers—blues and greens and purples—and when Cronk was seen against a light it shone through her feathers like an iridescent green hue. She had very dark really glittering eyes, quite large, and this

enormous bill that looked so destructive. It was designed for picking at carcases, because ravens are carrion-eaters. Scavengers, that is their job. Carcases
can be quite tough, and Cronk's beak was strong enough so that by using full
power she could crush your finger.

At nightfall Cronk would perch outside the back door in a window recess.
The window was beneath the inside stairs and every night going up to bed
Don would switch on the light and see this black figure, head tucked under its
wing, sleeping soundly. She would realise that Don was there and raise her
head and peer through the window. "Goodnight, Cronk . . ." and Don would
be gone upstairs.

THAT spring when visitors came to see Rufus, Cronk was always on the
scene. Eyes glittering, missing nothing. She had quickly realised who was the
centre of attention, and determined to try to take some of that attention for
herself. She deliberately showed off and flew to the top of the enclosure when
there was all this notice concentrated on Rufus. She would dart over and pull
at the women's hats, jump down and peck their ankles. There'd be pande-
monium for a while until they sorted themselves out, and Don or Meg would
try and control her behaviour. During all this Rufus would temporarily retire
from his performance—being scratched on his chest, posing for the photographers—and would lie, eyes closed, waiting for Cronk's antics to come to a
finish.

You couldn't imagine that he felt jealous of Cronk, that he experienced any
sense of being deprived of the spotlight. It was just that he was happy to let
his friend share in the fun. Only two or three times did Cronk take advantage
of the fact that he was protected by the wire-netting and catch Rufus a nip
in his tail. He would look annoyed at this and turn and make as if to bite her.
It was all part of the game. Cronk learned to imitate Shuna's bark. She
would perch on the roof and bark away down the chimney. You could hear
her bark reverberating through the house. There were buzzards down by the
loch and Cronk used to chase them away when they flew over the house,
barking at them like a dog.

One of Rufus's friends was a terrier who used to yap a lot outside the house.
It was the same terrier that had chased Cassius up the tree and nipped off
his tail. Cronk would deliberately tease the terrier. Rufus, Shuna and Cassius
—he would be up a tree—could look on at Cronk perched on the garden-
fence, barking back at the terrier in the road, which would go berserk with
fury and try to scramble up the fence to get at its tormentor. Cronk would

then hop down on to the road, the terrier would race after her, whereupon she would flutter above it just out of reach. From Cronk's point of view it was just for fun, but not with the terrier. It always tried to make it a bloodthirsty combat. But Cronk was always too quick for it.

By now, Don and Meg were taking Shuna, Cassius and Rufus into the forest. On the first outing Don thought it wisest to have Rufus on a lead, but after only a quarter-of-a-mile he took it off. There was obviously no need for it.

Cronk had to join in on these walks, of course. She would balance sometimes on Shuna's back, legs outstretched, holding on grimly. Then she would take off and fly ahead, waiting for the rest of the party to come along. Sometimes she would perch on Rufus's back, holding on tightly as she had done with Shuna. She never attempted to ride on Cassius's back, but would trot along beside him with that funny sideways hop she had. Growing tired of that she'd hop on to Shuna, who would trot on, tail wagging, this black apparition balancing on her back with wings outstretched. Then Cronk would take off to land on Rufus's back and go through the same performance. Now and again she would fly ahead, looking back at Don, impatient for him to hurry up.

She was forever picking up nails and bright pieces of stone and she'd hide them in the crevices in the rocks or in holes in tree-trunks. She would take moss from the rocks and cover the things that she'd hidden. Every time she went with the others back along the same forest path she would fly ahead to find and examine these treasures she'd hidden away. Fencing-staples—galvanised and bright in colour—were one of her favourite items. She was really addicted to fencing staples.

RUFUS was by nature too gentle to take advantage of the fact that Shuna was so easy to be put upon in the games they played. Cassius was sometimes quite rough with her, but she always took it in good part, and Cronk constantly teased her with his nips and barks. But even Rufus couldn't resist acting as Cronk's accomplice in a wonderful game she had devised. Shuna would always bring out her bone when it had just been given her, as if to show it off, whereupon Cronk would stalk her; Rufus at the crucial moment would distract her attention and Cronk would nip in, snatch the bone in her beak and fly off with it. Just a few yards, then she would drop it and wait for Shuna to dash up and retrieve it. Cronk would permit her to have a few gnaws, then stalk her again. Rufus would once more distract her attention at the crucial moment; she would drop the bone and again Cronk would "steal" it.

Cassius, naturally, wouldn't want to be left out of the game. When Shuna became wise to Rufus's part in the plot to make her let it go and refused to be distracted by him, Cassius would dash in to take her by surprise and, as before, Cronk would have the bone in his beak and be off with it. Shuna, of course, was always allowed to enjoy her bone in the end; in fact it came to it that she deliberately allowed herself to be the "victim" of the plot. Don and Meg and the children thought it as entertaining as any circus act.

Cronk had also extended her activities among the villagers themselves. She had already caused Catherine a certain amount of annoyance by following her when putting out the washing on the line and removing the pegs so that the clothes fell on to the ground, then she began visiting other gardens of the village. One neighbour, Mrs McInnes, was very fond of Cronk, but began to complain about the way she used to deal with her washing, especially as she picked on Mrs McInnes as a friend, flying over to see her in the morning.

Another game was with the village children when they were on their way to or from school, wearing their tam-o'-shanters with bobbins on them. Cronk would swoop from a chimney or roof-top, snatch the tammy and fly away with it. The child would think it had lost it forever, and the younger children would be very upset. They had to be reassured by Meg that Cronk would soon return the tammy safely. She always did.

One morning on his way to work Don noticed a raven high above the village. It wasn't Cronk, he knew; she was with Rufus, Shuna and Cassius. He watched the raven fly around for two or three minutes, then it went off in the direction of the forest. Later when he was in the forest he saw it again, flying high in the blue sky. Looking back on it, he recalls that even then he experienced a stab of intuition that there was some significance in the appearance of the raven.

Next morning he saw it again, circling high over the house as it had done the previous day. This time there was a sudden rush of wings and he saw Cronk fly up to meet the other raven. They flew together, circling high above the village, calling to each other and diving, then the strange raven headed for the forest again. Cronk flew back to the house, but later that day when he was in the forest Don saw it once more, and even as he watched it another raven joined it. Cronk. There was no doubt about it.

For several minutes he watched them circling and diving then went back to his office. At the back of his mind was a sense of unease. When he got back to the house at lunch-time there was no sign of Cronk. That afternoon he kept a look-out for both her and the other raven but they didn't appear again.

When he returned home that evening there was Cronk perched on the garden-gate waiting for him.

He gave a sigh of relief and bent his head to hers. She chattered to him, rubbing her black feathery cheek against his face. She was on his arm fluttering her wings at him in her familiar way as he went to the house. As he opened the door and called out to Catherine that Cronk was back she flew up to the roof.

But there still remained that niggling unease; he hadn't completely erased the picture of her and the other raven from his mind.

RUFUS STEALS THE SHOW
CHAPTER SEVEN

THE Highland Show is held in Edinburgh every year towards the end of June for three days. It's an international agricultural exhibition displaying equipment and livestock and for the 1969 event Don MacCaskill had been asked by the Royal Scottish Forestry Society to put on a wild-life display. He decided that Rufus might attract visitors, especially children.

He was required to be in Edinburgh the day before opening-day in order to check that an enclosure for Rufus had been properly prepared. Accordingly he set off that evening in the Dormobile with Rufus beside him on the driving-seat and also Shuna. He had no idea of putting her on show with Rufus. He had taken her along because she might get into mischief at home, since Catherine was busy with housework and couldn't keep an eye on her all the time. Besides, she would be company for Rufus.

Meg had to look after her mother when she was home from school, but she and the children saw Rufus the previous evening to wish him every success. Some of the children would see him at the show, because they would be going with their parents. But not Meg. Her parents couldn't afford it; Edinburgh was 150 miles away and it could have been the moon so far as Meg was concerned. She had never been away from the village.

Rufus and Shuna next to Don at the steering-wheel surveyed the scenery, but about twelve miles out, at the village of Taynuilt, Rufus was sick. Don put him out by the roadside. It had been a very winding road, or Rufus may have eaten something that had upset him; he shouldn't have been given any food the previous night. However, he managed to rid himself of whatever it was and the journey preceeded. A wee bit forlorn for a while, he curled up on the floor and Shuna got down from the driving seat to stretch herself out beside Rufus to comfort him. After about half-an-hour he perked up and sat next to Don again, Shuna beside him.

Reaching the top of the zig-zagging "Rest And Be Thankful" hill, Don stopped, took out his flask of tea and Rufus and Shuna accompanied him into the woods at the side of the road. A little burn ran down into the valley, and

while he enjoyed his tea Rufus and Shuna drank from the burn. The sky was cloudless and blue, the trees brilliant green and all around they heard the song of birds. Now he was on the last lap, and he reached Edinburgh's outskirts from the west through Linlithgow, along the Firth of Forth, branching off at Turnhouse Airport near where the show-park stands.

Rufus's enclosure was twelve foot by twelve, securely wire-netted, with a shelter for him to sleep in, and straw, food and water ready. Rufus settled in right away, as he was prepared to settle in anywhere, provided he was with someone he knew and trusted. Don put up the tent he had brought for himself to sleep in right beside the enclosure. It was an agricultural show, remember, attended largely by agricultural people, farmers, shepherds, gamekeepers and the like, to whom the sight of a fox could bring on an attack of such apoplectic hatred that they'd start looking for a gun. Someone might let Rufus loose again during the night, with the object of destroying him. Don wasn't taking any more risks than he could help. Shuna slept outside the tent, but next day, when the show opened, with the crowds starting right away to throng round Rufus's enclosure, Don couldn't leave Shuna tied up on her own. He put her in with Rufus. The result caused quite a stir. A fox and a

dog together, playing games as friendly as could be, a fox and a dog, supposed to be mortal enemies—the news spread so fast soon you could hardly get near. There were hundreds of people, mostly children dragging at their parents, clapping their hands and crying out, thrilled by the extraordinary sight. A fox and a dog together! Who would ever believe it?

The children scratched Rufus's chest through the wire-netting—Don allowed no one except news-photographers and a television camera-crew inside the enclosure—and he and Shuna played games while the children oohed and aahed and applauded. Rufus enjoyed it best when there was an opportunity to steal any piece of camera-equipment and dash off with it to the shelter, much to the onlookers' delight. And when the newsmen wanted to photograph him and Shuna together, one of them always contrived to be somewhere else just at the crucial moment before the click of the camera. Tame animals are usually worse than those in the wild to photograph—wild creatures who don't know you're there aren't self-conscious—and Rufus and Shuna made matters as awkward as they could.

Rufus enjoyed the first afternoon with the BBC television camera-crew best of all. Before anyone knew what was happening he had his head in the bag containing camera spares and was pulling out lenses—camera-lenses were always his favourite—and anything else he could lay his teeth on, whipping them off to the shelter. The crowd loved every moment of it. The television men managed to get control of the situation, order was restored and Rufus, backed up by Shuna, put all he knew into his performance before the camera. He appeared in a news-programme that same evening. Don wasn't able to see it, but he'd telephoned Catherine, who got in touch with Meg, whose parents didn't have television, to come along to the house. She was so thrilled at seeing Rufus, who needless to say looked as if he might have been a television-actor all his life, that when the programme ended she found herself crying. She couldn't help it, she wished so much she could be there with him. How dreadfully she missed him; it seemed so long since he had gone, and she counted the hours before he returned. That night she went home and wrote a special poem about him in the exercise-book she kept secretly in her bedroom.

There were photographs and new-stories about Rufus in the Scottish newspapers that evening and next day. His appearance was a great triumph, and all this publicity was drawing thousands more to the show, attendance figures were higher than ever. There was no doubt that this wonderful fox was the big attraction. But Don noticed that Rufus became tired and would

retire from showing off to the crowd and rest in the shelter two or three times during the day. Rather like a stage-star retiring to his dressing-room in between acts. Shuna, though much more placid, duly followed suit. They would lie down together and take a breather. He observed something else also. Something which bothered him, though he couldn't tell why. A curious look of abstraction on Rufus's face, as if his thoughts were somewhere else, somewhere far away. No doubt, Don decided, being so close to this crowd was proving a bit of a strain, causing a certain amount of tension. Don, too, felt the strain, having to be on the alert all the time for any fox-hater or clumsy member of the throng trying to poke at Rufus with his walking-stick.

And there was the woman, who cool as you please, wanted to buy him, almost demanded it, because, as she explained, the district where she hunted was temporarily short of foxes. There was the shepherd who barged up and harangued him for daring to keep a tame fox, when it ought to have been destroyed at birth—if it wasn't for people like Don there wouldn't be such bluidy vermin all over the place killing sheep. He hadn't realised, Don

replied, that there were all that number trying to protect foxes, but if there were he was glad to hear it. Of course, you couldn't get through to a chap like that. You just tried not to lose your temper with him. But after three days of thousands of folk milling around his nerves were slightly tattered and episodes like this left a nasty taste in the mouth, so that when Friday came and it was time to pack up and go home he experienced a sense of relief. Deep down he couldn't help feeling that he had allowed Rufus to be exploited, when he ought to have had his interest really at heart. He should be planning to return him to the wild, where he belonged.

It was ten o'clock and growing dark when the Dormobile reached Inverinan. Catherine, with Cassius and Meg were waiting at the gate and Meg took Rufus in her arms. He nuzzled his face against hers and she smelled the wonderful musky scent of him. Followed by Shuna and Cassius, purring a welcome and arching his back against his legs, Don and his wife went into the house. Meg took Rufus to the enclosure, put him inside and carefully padlocked the gate. He stared up at her though the wire-netting, wagging his tail. She had a chokiness in her throat now that he was back. "Goodnight, Rufus . . ." He twitched his brush and went slowly over to his den.

Meg returned to the house with the padlock-key. Don turned as she came in and told her what Catherine had just told him. Cronk was missing. He had flown off in the afternoon and not returned.

Don remembered the other raven, and that intuition he'd had.

THE INVALID
CHAPTER EIGHT

MEG thought that perhaps it was because Cronk was jealous at Don going off to Edinburgh with Rufus and Shuna and leaving her behind. But Don knew it wasn't that; it was inevitable that she should go, and he was glad. It was natural for her to have flown away, to find a mate. It was as it should be, it was Life, and he felt happy for her and grateful for the wonderful memories she had left behind. And the inexorable call she had answered served to underscore for him the responsibility he owed Rufus. It was fast approaching, the decision he would have to make to let him go. For several days after Cronk had vanished he kept a look-out for her and the other raven, but so far as he knew he never saw them, never again heard Cronk barking in the sky.

It must have been a couple of weeks since his return from his Edinburgh triumph that Rufus started to go off his food and began to appear ill. His eyes were dull, his attitude listless, he looked thin and out of condition. Don re-called his attack of sickness on the way to Edinburgh, but he had apparently completely recovered from it; had he picked up an infection during the show, or had someone managed to administer poison to him? He wasn't being sick, however, so the indications were that if it had been poison he'd got rid of it; but he was certainly shivering, nose and eyes were running; perhaps it was a chill, some sort of influenza. It was essential to keep him warm, and he brought him into the house, found a dog-basket, padded it with blankets and Rufus lay in it, well out of the way of draughts on the hearth-rug, wrapped in a tartan shawl and looking very sorry for himself. He was sufficiently house-trained to make the effort to stagger out of his basket to where a piece of newspaper was placed for him in a corner. Then he would make his way very mournfully, slowly back to his basket and wait for his shawl to be wrapped round him again. He would lower himself almost out of sight, covered with the shawl and only the tip of his nose showing.

Shuna and Cassius showed their sympathy, nuzzling him and licking his face and doing their best to revive his spirits, but there was no improvement and after three days Don decided to get help from David Stephen in Glasgow.

At the end of Don's account on the telephone of his symptoms, Stephen thought it might be a case of poisoning, or some infection picked up, probably at Edinburgh. But he said he'd know better if he came over and gave Rufus a proper examination. He was very interested in Rufus and anxious for his welfare.

He arrived next afternoon, took a careful look at Rufus and diagnosed what was known as German, or Continental, distemper, a less virulent type of distemper which ordinarily afflicts dogs. How he'd come by it couldn't be said; as he'd suggested earlier, it might have been at the show, or from a local dog, though Don hadn't heard of any dog in the village being ill. Shuna had been inoculated against the disease as a pup, so she was in no danger. Stephen was a firm believer in herbal remedies in the case of a sick animal—animals instinctively know what herbs or berries possess the appropriate curative properties: a cat or dog, for example, eats a special kind of grass when in need of an emetic—and Rufus would have found a cure for himself in the wild. He duly prescribed some tincture of belladonna (obtained from deadly nightshade), together with a bismuth compound and pepsin, plus cascara. A teaspoonful of the medicine four times daily. He felt confident there was every chance of the patient making a complete recovery.

Don and Meg took it in turn to administer the medicine, which Rufus downed without too much fuss. Shuna mothered him while Cassius lent his moral support, the two of them nuzzling him and licking his face to express their sympathy and, you might say, willing him to get better. Almost from the first spoonful he began to perk up, his eyes brightened, he wanted to eat. The village children had called every day to inquire after him and now that the news was better they brought his favourite "Snowballs", but he wasn't allowed them yet. By the end of the week Don was able to report to David Stephen that his medicine had done the trick.

Stephen had also prescribed egg-flip and Amontillado sherry, and this Rufus took to at once—raw egg and sherry was one thing about being an invalid that he did enjoy, together with the attention he received. In his shawl and huddled in his basket he looked the part to perfection, perking up when his egg and sherry was due and warmly responding to the love and care heaped upon him.

By the beginning of August Rufus was well enough to give up his basket on the hearth and was taken back to his enclosure. He expressed his joy at returning to his old home by leaping into the air in that way he had and racing round from corner to corner exploring his territory; he dived into his den to reappear from the other exit, dived back again and came out the way he'd first gone in. Meg produced the old tennis-ball and he was playing his usual pouncing game. Shuna and Cassius were joining in, and the local children came along. When the grocer's van stopped outside he was allowed to scoff the "Snowballs" and was soon wearing that comical white moustache.

It was just like old times. Except that he didn't settle down quite the same as he had before, and Don still thought he sometimes had that strange abstracted look. As the summer came to its end it seemed to Don that he had begun to become more withdrawn. Finally he made up his mind to pretend to Meg that Rufus had once more escaped. He simply couldn't find it in himself to tell her he meant deliberately to set him free. Much better for her to think that Rufus had gone of his own accord, the same way that Cronk had gone.

THE end of September.

The best place to release him was where he would stand every chance of getting food for himself easily. Don would be putting some out for him at the release-point for the first few days, so that he wouldn't starve while he was getting his bearings—to begin with he wouldn't be used to hunting, but he would quickly get the hang of it, it was instinctive to him. The time of the year was right, the time when the young cub in the wild leaves its parents and goes out into the world on his own—which could perhaps explain the feeling of abstraction about him Don had sensed.

Early one dawn Don left the house and went to the enclosure. He opened the gate as Rufus came over to him as he would have done ordinarily, chattering a welcome. Don picked him up and took him to the car.

Loch Awe was reflecting a sky beginning to grow pink as Don reached the shore. Behind him stretched the forest into the last grey remains of the night. When it came to the point, he could hardly bring himself to take Rufus out of the car. He nearly made up his mind not to go through with it, but to take him back. He held him tightly a few moments more then put him down. Rufus simply stood there looking at him, making no attempt to move. Don made as if to pick him up again but this time the fox moved away a few steps. Then he looked back at Don as if asking him to follow him. Don stood and watched. Rufus trotted along the shore and paused again. Again he looked

back as if waiting for Don to come after him. As if it were a new game he was expected to play. Don stood still. Rufus took a drink from the loch as the water lapped his paws. Don just left him to it and got into the car, looking back to where Rufus was staring out across the loch as it glittered in the morning light. There were little splashes of silver as he began to trot along the edge of the water. Don got into the car and blew his nose hard. Then he pushed his handkerchief back into his pocket and drove off.

He had left food for Rufus by the side of the loch so that he would be all right for that day, and he would come back that evening and leave more —dried meat and rabbit—in the same place.

He went back to bed, but hardly slept; Catherine, who had woken up, didn't get much sleep either. At about six o'clock he got up to make a pot of tea. Catherine had at last fallen asleep and he went downstairs as quietly as he could. It was just as he had the kettle on that there came a knocking at the back door. It was Meg standing there. She was holding Rufus in her arms. "He's escaped," she said.

Don stared at her open-mouthed. Clutching Rufus in her arms, she came into the kitchen. He closed the door after her, still unable to say anything. While Rufus was licking her face, Meg was explaining how she had got up as usual and opened the back door to get the milk, and there he was, sitting on the doorstep. He had jumped into her arms and she, in astonishment, nearly dropped the bottle of milk. Without telling her parents, she had hurried along with him through the early morning mist, and now she must get back otherwise her parents would be wondering what had happened to her.

Don held Rufus while he licked his face and chattered to him in his inimitable way.

Catherine had heard their voices and came downstairs just as Meg left. She really could hardly believe her eyes as she saw Rufus. Don just let the tears run down his face.

FRIEDA
CHAPTER NINE

D ON headed back to Inverinan from Airdrie with the vixen David Stephen had given him in a crate in the back of the Dormobile. Stephen had recently acquired her from the Royal Scottish Society for the Prevention of Cruelty to Animals; she was a year old and had grown too big for her original owner who had her as a cub. It was three weeks after Rufus's return and he had settled down again after his brief adventure, though his attitude towards Don had been a little wary at first.

Don realised that he had misinterpreted Rufus's needs, that he had grown too tame, the bond between him and human beings had become unbreakable, he was caught between the human world and the wild. Don also realised that it still remained his responsibility to provide Rufus with some bridge by which means he could cross from one world to the other and back again. The answer, Don was certain, was to find him a mate, and he had got in touch with Stephen. The result was now in the back of the Dormobile. Her name was Frieda, and she was a different proposition altogether from Rufus. She was smaller in size and nothing like so friendly as Rufus had been. She had almost cowered when Don first met her, and appeared apprehensive of him. Stephen himself had been able to handle her, but he explained that she had got on well with his two dogs.

He was half way on the road home when suddenly from the corner of his eye he saw Frieda sitting beside him. Stephen hadn't secured the crate-door properly, so that she had been able to put her nose under it and lift it up. Don promptly braked and considered putting her back into the crate, though he knew he would risk being bitten. But it wasn't only because he was afraid of being bitten that he hesitated: you can never be on the same terms with an animal once it's taken a bite at you. It's always best to prevent it happening at all. Should he try to shift her or leave her alone? He drove on and she continued to sit there. After a couple of miles she jumped down and quietly returned to the crate. It was as if it was her home, and there is this about an animal—if it decides that wherever it happens to find itself is its home, then

it'll want to go back to that particular place.

It was dark when Don reached Inverinan. He couldn't foresee how Rufus would react to Frieda at their first meeting, or she to him, so he wouldn't put her in the enclosure straight away. Instead, she could spend the night in the shed at the back of the house, and introductions made next morning. He prepared a corner for her with plenty of straw, food and water, let her out of the crate, which he left for her in case she preferred to go back to it, and carefully locked the shed-door behind him.

Next morning she was out of the crate and he couldn't get her back into it in order to transport her to the enclosure. She went into a corner, raising her lip at him and snarling. If he attempted to pick her up and carry her bodily she would struggle, bite and escape. She had decided the corner of the shed was her home, and here she wanted to remain, but after several minutes of talking to her quietly and shifting the crate into another position, he managed to persuade her to get back into it.

Rufus got her scent the moment he approached the enclosure and was at the gate as Don went in. He put it down and opened the crate-door. Frieda came out at once, and for one heart-stopping moment Don thought she was going to attack Rufus. But he put his nose up to her in his usual, friendly way and soon they were both wagging their tails.

Don sat on the crate and watched them. Rufus followed Frieda around, sniffing at her like a dog at a bitch. She seemed quite happy to be with him and they settled down together, licking each other's faces.

At the beginning of his relationship with Frieda, Rufus may have paid less attention to Don than usual, but his affection towards Meg never wavered. Frieda however, always kept herself very much to herself. Once she had sorted out the territory-bounds of the enclosure and the den, her attitude was remote. Even Rufus in his most abstracted mood was a hundred times more friendly than she was. Meg and the children were very excited at watching the vixen with Rufus, but she soon took herself off, usually to the den, where she seemed to remain most of the day; Don observed that she was more active above ground at night-time.

Not for her the "Snowballs" that Rufus gobbled up, and whereas he still stood up against the fence to allow his chest to be scratched with evident bliss, still posed for his photograph and went through his performances with the old tennis-ball, she seemed anxious not to be noticed; and, as Meg at once observed, she didn't possess the same round, innocent eyes that were such a marked feature of Rufus. But Don knew that Rufus was happy, as

happy as he could ever be. Frieda formed the bridge he needed between his life with human beings and that of the wild. There were still the games and companionship with Shuna and Cassius; he came often to the house to share the hearth with them. He played games in the garden with Meg and the children as well as the passing tourists who came to see him in increasing numbers as his fame continued to spread. At these times Frieda invariably remained down in the den. The presence of people didn't seem to distress or upset her, she just didn't show any interest in them, and Don was satisfied that she wasn't suffering any harm as a result of Rufus's popularity. She lived her own life.

She ate at the same time as he did, and kept up a communication with him; and he made an understanding mate, never intruding on her solitariness. Just as he had solved the problem of leading a nocturnal existence on the one hand and sharing day-time hours with Don and Meg and the others, so now he took part appropriately in Frieda's life. This was what struck Don as representing perhaps his most extraordinary and endearing trait—his desire and ability to divide his life in the way he had.

Towards Shuna, Frieda was reasonably friendly; she was a female and anyway she had been friendly with David Stephen's dogs; but it wasn't the same where Cassius was concerned: Cassius took one sniff at her from a safe distance through the wire-netting, turned his back and went his way. Frieda no doubt reciprocated his sentiments.

As winter came, Rufus warmed again towards Don; it was as if he had learned to appreciate what had been done for him and was determined to express his love as fully as he could. The snow fell more heavily that year, which gave him splendid opportunities for playing games with Frieda, and they raced round the enclosure, sending the snow flying. When Don came to watch them, Rufus would deliberately race up to him, stopping short to cover him in a shower of snow. Don would reciprocate by chasing Rufus and showering snow on him. They played some good games in the snow together, and it didn't matter if Frieda refused to join in; Rufus was demonstrating his love for Don.

FOXES breed once a year and the vixen comes into heat around February, when she barks and calls with that strange screeching call at night. Frieda conformed to pattern and Don had a faint hope that she and Rufus would mate, though it was unusual for foxes to do so in captivity. Frieda was only a

year old, which he thought might be a bit young for her, especially as she still seemed rather unsettled in her present environment. But he'd forgotten what a very special fox her mate was.

Don witnessed Rufus and Frieda mating on February the 19th, 1970. Would she give birth to cubs, would he have the opportunity which had been denied him when he tried to observe from his hide in the forest what went on between the parents and their cubs?

He realised that Frieda had reached the first stages of pregnancy when one day he saw her pulling the fur away from her teats. She was beginning to look thinner round the flanks, he thought, then realised that in fact her belly was becoming larger. Her head seemed smaller on her body and she was appearing even less frequently in the enclosure and spending increasingly more time in the den. At the sight of anyone, even Don or Meg, she would slink off—that was the best way you could describe it—underground. She behaved like this until it came to the time when she was never leaving the den.

Don made no attempt to disturb her or even try to look at her. He kept away, and, of course, so did Meg. The danger of disturbing her when she gave birth to her cubs was that she could easily destroy them. The gestation period is about fifty-two days, so you could work out the date when they where expected to arrive, but it's much safer to wait at least a fortnight after the date when they're due before risking a look to see how the mother and young are doing. Don's job was to see that Rufus was provided with the food to take to Frieda.

Of course, Meg had been on tiptoe with suspense, and also the children, when Don told them that according to his calculations he thought Frieda had given birth to the cubs. Whenever Meg or the children came to see Rufus he was always brought out into the garden, and Meg would see that everyone dropped their voices so as not to disturb Frieda. Shuna, too, and Cassius weren't allowed to spend as much time in the enclosure as they had done, though Rufus came into the house with them frequently.

It was just over two weeks after the date Don had calculated she must have had her cubs that he saw her come up for the food Rufus had put for her. There was a lot more fur away from her teats, and there was the moisture of milk on them. The cubs were there.

They would be tiny black things, a few inches long, born blind, their eyes not opening for fourteen or fifteen days. She would suckle them underground until they were a month old. Then they would be allowed out of the den. As the time approached when they would emerge, Rufus began calling them. It wasn't like his ecstatic chattering with which he greeted Don and Meg, but a low-pitched wuffling; it was meant to entice the cubs out, to get them to come out and take a look at the world about them. There's nothing more curious than a newly-born fox-cub.

One morning on his way to the office Don heard Rufus calling, more loudly, more insistently and enticingly it seemed to him. He went to the enclosure. Sure enough, there they were just coming out into daylight for the first time. Two of them. He didn't go into the enclosure but remained outside watching. Frieda appeared, keeping her eye on them and seeing that Rufus didn't get too near them. Don saw her show him the curl of her lip when he did make a move towards them. He couldn't help experiencing a chokiness in his throat as he saw the two young cubs. The litter usually numbers three or four or

even five, but he concluded that perhaps it was because she was so young that she had given birth only to two.

Now their coats had changed to a smoky colour. He could see clearly their opened eyes, they were bright blue, absolutely brilliant blue. Their expressions were enigmatic, both of them immediately saw him as he stood there and they stared at him intently, not a muscle in their tiny bodies moving. Their faces at this age were not at all fox-shaped; they didn't have the long nose of the fox, it was a sort of squat face with a very short nose. They didn't look like foxes at all.

Don was very pleased at the cubs' arrival, not only because it is rare for the fox to breed in captivity but because he would have many opportunities to photograph and to study them and the pattern of their behaviour with the

parents. It would compensate for the failure of his hide in the forest. He intended that the cubs wouldn't be tamed any more than Frieda had been; he wanted them to grow as free as they could in the circumstances and in the environment which had been provided for them. This was important for the field study he planned. Observing the cubs in the enclosure would offer him if not exactly a short-cut at least clues upon which he could deduce reasonably accurately what were the real conditions under which foxes lived in the wild.

In their natural state, Don had observed in the past, the cubs would be fed in the morning or in the evening, depending upon when the dog-fox kills and supplies the food to the vixen. He knew what was the required intake of food for the cubs, plus Frieda and plus Rufus, and he prepared that amount which he fed to Rufus every evening when he got back from the forest. It was the forest which made up the menu: dead rabbits, dead birds, rats and mice. He fed Rufus and Frieda on dried meat, but never tried that for the cubs to start with, because dried meat is too hard and their teeth are not fully developed.

Don learned later that Frieda had burrowed into the floor of the den. He hadn't wire-netted the floor when he'd built it, and she'd had the bare earth into which she had tunnelled her way for nearly ten feet. She had never allowed Rufus to go into this freshly made tunnel, it was the raised lip at him and the snarl.

When, however, the cubs came up from below ground Frieda began handing over some of the responsibility for their care to Rufus. In fact, as Don pointed out to Meg, she was by degrees retreating into the background, until by August she was having almost nothing whatever to do with the cubs. She would lie in a corner or even climb the tree and lie on the topmost branch, where the cubs couldn't reach her. If one did get near to her, of course, it would attempt to suckle her, and by now its teeth were very sharp and extremely painful for Frieda.

So Rufus virtually took over her job. He gave less time to entertaining the children and visitors—they weren't allowed near the enclosure during this time—to spend hours playing games with the cubs. Hide-and-seek and chasing each other, and, of course, the pouncing game with Meg's old tennis-ball. But always Don and Meg noticed that he never allowed a cub to stray too far away from the den; he would quickly catch it and bring it back. He was as loving and gentle as any father could be.

Summer had turned the corner into Autumn; Don noted that the cubs, one of which was a dog-fox and the other a vixen, were beginning to go off individually to search out what lay beyond the area round their den, and Rufus was less inclined to fetch them back. They were becoming old enough to fend for themselves; soon they would want to go off on their own, live their own lives.

That October Don was offered the job of head forester at Tummel Forest, Pitlochry, Perthshire. He would be leaving Inverinan the following month.

GOOD-BYE?
CHAPTER TEN

IF the move to Pitlochry meant a momentous upheaval for Don and Catherine, what did it mean to Meg? It spelled good-bye to Rufus; she would be fortunate if she ever saw him again. Pitlochry is sixty miles of narrow, winding roads from Inverinan and half-a-day away, remote and isolated, with no rail and buses few and far between, and anyway the fare was impossibly expensive for her, even if her father or mother would allow her to go. Don was so dismayed at the thought of having to break the news that his wife offered to do it for him. But it was up to him to tell her. If Catherine was there, it would help.

That evening when she came round as usual, he told her. At first she couldn't really comprehend what it meant. The end of her friendship with Rufus whom she had come to love so dearly, who had become part of her life, about whom she wrote her poems and thought of almost all the time. . . . He would be gone. Don and Catherine tried to reassure her by suggesting she talked with her father; perhaps she could talk him round, get him to agree to allow her to come and see Rufus. But she was certain he wouldn't think of it, and as for giving her the fare for the journey—it was something she couldn't bring herself to ask him. She would be talking about something which he was incapable of understanding—his hatred for the pestilent vermin hadn't diminished just because he'd been indulgent about her making friends with MacCaskill's bluidy fox.

Next evening, however, she had wonderful news. She rushed in to tell Don that she had managed to summon up courage to speak to her father; she'd told him Rufus was going and pleaded to be allowed to visit him, at least later, after Christmas perhaps. She had begged with all her heart—and he relented, agreed that she could go, and that he would give her the bus-fare. Don and Catherine were tremendously pleased for her.

She went to see Rufus, to hold him close. He chattered to her and licked her happy tears away, appearing to understand that everything was going to be all right after all.

Don wasn't taking the cubs. He had discussed with David Stephen what should be the proper course and it was decided they should be released, given their chance in the wild. As Don had managed to put in a considerable amount of study of them in their family life, made photographs as required, and all along scrupulously avoided any attempt to tame them, intending that they should be freed, now was the time. The place would be a wild-life reserve near Loch Lomond. Stephen would come over to help him; the young cubs would have to be caught and transported to the release-point.

Don told Catherine, but no one else, and one evening two weeks before their departure for Pitlochry Stephen arrived and they went into the enclosure. At their approach both cubs dived into the den. Frieda had no interest in them and went off to a corner on her own, while Rufus was persuaded to keep out of the way. Don and Stephen set to and dug the cubs out. It was the only way to get them; they were wild and instinctively scared of human beings. They dug down to where they huddled together at the end of Frieda's burrow and grabbed them by the tail. That's the way to catch a young fox, by the root of the brush, then get your hand to the nape of its neck, so it can't turn and bite you. They put them into a big crate Don had made and went off in the Dormobile, putting in some rabbit and dried meat.

Two hours later they reached the wild-life reserve and on the shore of the loch got the crate out and waited for the pair to show themselves. They didn't want to come out, because by this time, even after such a short journey, the crate was their home. It was quite a job, but after shooing them, banging on the crate, then tipping it a little, the young dog-fox poked out his head very cautiously and looked around. Then he became bolder and came right out, sniffing with his nose in the air. It was about seven o'clock, dusk, owls were hooting and the waves were lapping the shore. He trotted along the shore a little way then came back and invited his sister to appear. She came out and went up to him. Their eyes were the same shape as those of their mother, not round and innocent like Rufus's, but their fur was as dark as his. They were very rangy-looking.

They turned together away from the shore and jumped on to a bank to disappear into the trees. Don had put the food down before they left the crate so that they actually passed it. They knew it was there. He and Stephen took the crate and drove home. Every night for a week Don took food to the release-point. The last evening he found it still where he had left it, they hadn't needed to come for it; they were hunting successfully for themselves. They could look after themselves, now. Perhaps they would stay together,

even mate and have cubs of their own. He liked to think they would, that they would elude their enemies.

The evening arrived when Meg held Rufus in her arms for the last time for what she knew must be months to come. She would be at school next morning when the Dormobile left; for that reason the children had said their good-byes to Don and Catherine, Rufus, Frieda, Shuna and Cassius on their way home that afternoon. Meg wanted to say good-bye on her own and Don left her alone with Rufus in the enclosure.

Don and Catherine were careful to look at Meg very casually when she came back to the house. But she wasn't crying, there were no tear-stains on her face, and when Don went with her to the garden-gate she still held back her tears. He watched her as she disappeared into the evening dusk. She walked slowly and he stood looking after her several moments when she was out of sight.

THE road from Pitlochry, the little town surrounded by the sheltering hills, branches off over Garry Bridge and winds up towards the forest. Beside the forest, Don's and Catherine's new home was a low-built white house, a large garden in front, behind it offices and out-buildings. Down from the back ran a lightly wooded slope and it was here that he had built Rufus's and Frieda's enclosure. He had planned and set it up while he was waiting to move in and it was all ready when they arrived, four times the size of the one at Inverinan, strongly wire-netted top and sides; and he had dug a splendid den, most natural-looking. There was a bench for Rufus and several small trees for Frieda to climb.

The location was very popular with tourists, especially in the summer. Don realised there would be crowds who would want to watch Rufus, but the experience at Edinburgh had made him wary against putting him on show again. For another thing, he couldn't be sure what sort of reaction there would be among local people when it became known that he kept Rufus and Frieda. He couldn't rule out the probability that attempts would be made to kill them. There was little doubt that there were as many round about who hated foxes as implacably as those at Inverinan. Accordingly he had built the enclosure so that it was screened by the rise of the land and trees from the road tourists used.

Winter came and you could see on the crisp, clear days the icy mountain-tops of Glencoe to the distant west; and the snows passed, Rufus happy in his new home with plenty of space to move around. From his bench he could enjoy the loch and forest below. He had his friends, Don, Shuna and Cassius, and was soon sharing the new sitting-room hearth with them as often as ever. And with Frieda, of course, who spent her time much as before, keeping herself to herself; they would mate in the Spring and Don would be able to continue his studies of the fox's life-history.

Early in February 1971, Meg came home from school one afternoon, to be met at the door by a neighbour. The doctor was there: her father had died suddenly of a heart-attack and her mother was in a state of collapse from shock.

It took Meg several weeks to get over that dreadful afternoon. She was able to write a brief letter to Don and Catherine, who had heard that Joe Allan had died, and she asked after Rufus, sending him her love. She told them she had to look after her mother. Already ailing, she was now as a result of her husband's death depressively ill. It meant that for Meg to leave her for any length of time was impossible.

She wrote every now and again, always asking after Rufus. There seemed little chance of her being able to come to see Rufus in the foreseeable future and at the end of May Don felt that he ought to try and persuade Jean Allen to allow Meg a few hours off. He set off on the narrow winding road to Inverinan and when he met her mother she agreed that Meg could go back with him for the afternoon. Meg was full of excitement, although frightened that after so long Rufus wouldn't remember her.

She was greeted by Catherine and Shuna, who wagged her tail with delight at seeing her again, while Cassius arched his back against her, purring away. Don took her down to the enclosure. Rufus was by the gate and he looked up at their approach. Suddenly he caught Meg's scent and froze momentarily, then he leapt up against the fence, chattering with ecstasy. Meg could barely speak to him she was so choked with tears. She went in; Rufus, jumping up and down with joy, leapt into her arms, and she smelled his familiar, warm musky smell as he nuzzled her and licked her face.

She stayed with him all afternoon. She had brought the old tennis-ball, which had been hidden away with her excerise-book of poems, and he played his old pouncing game, just as it was at Inverinan. Frieda hadn't shown her-self at all, but stayed in a corner down the slope. Rufus came in with Meg at tea-time and sat next to her, while Shuna and Cassius joined the party.

It was getting late, Meg had promised to be home before darkness. She and Rufus went back to the enclosure. Don waited for her in the car and presently she brought the key to the enclosure-gate which she had carefully locked after her. She got into the car and Don drove off back to Inverinan. She said very little on the way and he didn't encourage her to talk. He knew her heart was too full.

As they approached the village, where lights were beginning to show in the windows, Don said "You'll come again some day. . . ."

She looked up at him with a quick, hopeful smile.